YOU SHOULD MEET Shirley Chisholm

by Laurie Calkhoven

illustrated by Kaitlyn Shea O'Connor

Ready-to-Read

Simon Spotlight
New York London Toronto Sydney New Delhi

SIMON SPOTLIGHT
An imprint of Simon & Schuster Children's Publishing Division
1230 Avenue of the Americas, New York, New York 10020
This Simon Spotlight edition May 2020
Text copyright © 2020 by Simon & Schuster, Inc.
Illustrations copyright © 2020 by Kaitlyn Shea O'Connor
For information about special discounts for bulk purchases, please contact Simon & Schuster Special Sales at
1-866-506-1949 or business@simonandschuster.com
Manufactured in the United States of America 0420 LAK
2 4 6 8 10 9 7 5 3 1
Library of Congress Cataloging-in-Publication Data
Names: Calkhoven, Laurie, author. | O'Connor, Kaitlyn Shea, illustrator.
Title: Shirley Chisholm / by Laurie Calkhoven ; illustrated by Kaitlyn Shea O'Connor.
Description: New York : Simon Spotlight, Inc., 2020. | Series: You should meet | Audience: Ages 6–8 | Audience:
Grades 2–3 | Summary: "A ready-to-read level 3 biography of Shirley Chisholm, who, in 1972, became the first
African American woman to enter the Democratic presidential race in the United States"—Provided by publisher.
Identifiers: LCCN 2020000880 (print) | LCCN 2020000881 (eBook) | ISBN 9781534465572 (paperback) |
ISBN 9781534465589 (hardcover) | ISBN 9781534465596 (eBook)
Subjects: LCSH: Chisholm, Shirley, 1924-2005—Juvenile literature. | African American legislators—United
States—Biography—Juvenile literature. | Women legislators—United States—Biography—Juvenile literature. |
African American women—Biography—Juvenile literature. | Presidential candidates—United States—
Biography—Juvenile literature. | United States. Congress. House—Biography—Juvenile literature.
Classification: LCC E840.8.C48 C35 2021 (print) | LCC E840.8.C48 (eBook) | DDC 328.73/092 [B]—dc23
LC record available at https://lccn.loc.gov/2020000880
LC ebook record available at https://lccn.loc.gov/2020000881

CONTENTS

Introduction   5

Chapter 1: Brooklyn and Barbados   9

Chapter 2: College and Career   17

Chapter 3: "Unbought and Unbossed"   21

Chapter 4: "Candidate of the People"   33

Chapter 5: Dare to Dream   37

But Wait . . . There's More!   41

Introduction

Have you ever dared to dream when people said you shouldn't even try? Have you fought for something you believed in? Maybe you have a secret dream or goal that you think is too impossible to ever achieve.

If any of those things are true of you, then you should meet Shirley Chisholm. Shirley Chisholm was the first African American woman ever elected to Congress. She was also the first African American person, male or female, to seek the nomination for president of the United States from either the Democratic or Republican party (the two major political parties in America).

Shirley didn't win, but she opened the door for women and for African Americans who came after her. A lot of politicians wanted Shirley to stay out of public life. But she wouldn't. She famously said, "If they don't give you a seat at the table, bring a folding chair."

When she was asked why she ran for president, she answered, "Why not? Why not dare to dream?"

Once you meet Shirley, you'll be inspired to dare to dream too!

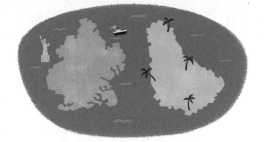

Chapter 1
Brooklyn and Barbados

Shirley Anita St. Hill was born in Brooklyn, New York, on November 30, 1924. Her mother was from Barbados. Her father was a factory laborer from Guyana. Times were hard for the family, and Shirley's parents wanted the best for her and her two younger sisters. When Shirley was three years old, they made the decision to bring the girls to Barbados. Shirley and her sisters lived on a farm with their grandmother while their parents struggled to earn a living in Brooklyn.

Shirley missed her parents, but she later said, "Granny gave me strength, dignity, and love. I learned from an early age that I was somebody." Shirley went to school in a one-room schoolhouse. It was a strict school, but she learned to read and write easily. After school each day, she and her sisters did chores on the farm. They collected eggs from the chickens and ducks, and fed the cows, sheep, and goats. Shirley learned to take pride in her work on the farm. When their chores were done, the girls also played and swam at the island's beaches.

About seven years later, Shirley left the peaceful island for the busy streets of Brooklyn. It was the Great Depression—a time when many people struggled to find work—but Shirley's parents wanted their children with them. Her father worked in a factory and a bakery. Her mother was a seamstress and cleaned other people's houses. They were poor, but they were together.

In school, Shirley was placed in a lower grade because she hadn't been taught American history in Barbados. She started to cause trouble in class. It wasn't long before her teachers realized she was bored and should be in a higher grade. From then on, she was a great student.

Shirley's father loved to read. He read the newspapers every day and was always reading books. He inspired Shirley to love reading too. He talked about politics at the dinner table, and encouraged his daughters to be interested in government. Her mother wanted all the girls to go to college.

Shirley graduated from Brooklyn Girls' High School in 1942. Her grades earned her scholarships to top colleges, but those scholarships didn't pay for room and board. She decided to live at home and go to Brooklyn College.

Chapter 2
College and Career

Shirley studied sociology at Brooklyn College and thought she would like to be a teacher. She won prizes for debating. A **debate** is a formal discussion in which people argue different sides of the same question. Shirley's professors told her that her debate skills would serve her well in politics.

When she graduated from Brooklyn College in 1946, Shirley began working as a preschool teacher. At the same time, she studied for her master's degree at Columbia University. She also met and married Conrad Chisholm.

At home in Brooklyn, Shirley got involved in local politics. She joined Democratic clubs and worked to help black candidates get elected to local offices. Then, after years of helping other people get elected, Shirley decided to run for office herself. In 1964, she was elected to the New York State Assembly. She was one of just four women in the assembly, and she

worked to pass bills to increase funding for day care and to help working people.

Shirley was a success and won the respect of the people she represented in Brooklyn. It wasn't long before she began to think about a higher office—the United States Congress.

Chapter 3
"Unbought and Unbossed"

In the late 1960s, supporters asked Shirley
to run for the United States Congress.
A race to win a seat in the House of
Representatives would be long and hard.
Shirley wasn't convinced she should run.
One night, a poor woman came to her door
in Brooklyn and said she and her friends
wanted Shirley to be their candidate. "She
gave me a dirty envelope containing $9.62
in nickels, dimes, and quarters," Shirley
said. The woman promised to raise money
every week, and Shirley promised to run.

Shirley never had as much money as the men she ran against, but she ran a new kind of campaign. She spoke to the women voters in her district, something the other candidates never did. She also spoke Spanish to her Spanish-speaking neighbors and encouraged everyone to register to vote. She drove through her neighborhood in a truck and spoke through a loudspeaker. "I'm 'Fighting Shirley Chisholm,'" she told them. She wanted people to know she would stick up for them and fight for them. And she asked them to vote for her.

Shirley told the voters that she was "unbought and unbossed." That meant she hadn't taken money from big corporations and that no one could tell her what to do. "Unbought and Unbossed" became Shirley's campaign slogan, or motto, for the rest of her career. And she always made sure that it was true.

Not only did Shirley win in the 1968 election, but she also became the first African American woman elected to Congress. All of a sudden, she was famous. Everyone wanted to know more about her. Shirley made her mark right away by hiring an all-female staff to work in her Washington, DC, office.

DAILY PRESS

Shirley Chisholm Will Not Be Silenced

The United States faced a lot of challenges in 1968. In that year civil rights leader Martin Luther King Jr. and presidential candidate Robert F. Kennedy were both killed. The country was also fighting an unpopular war in Vietnam.

The men in Congress expected Shirley to take a back seat. They expected her to be quiet and not voice her opinions. She was a newcomer and needed to pay her dues. That meant other representatives in Congress who had been there longer than Shirley got their requests answered first. But the woman who called herself "Fighting Shirley Chisholm" was never good at taking a back seat. Representatives in Congress are assigned to committees—groups that work together on different issues. Shirley was assigned to the Agriculture Committee. There were no farms in Brooklyn, and Shirley asked to be reassigned.

No one could believe that Shirley was making this request! Only people who had been in Congress for a long time got to choose the best committees. But Shirley didn't give up. She was finally reassigned to the Veterans' Affairs Committee. "There are a lot more veterans in my district than trees," she joked.

That committee gave Shirley a chance to improve life for United States veterans— people who have served in the air force, army, navy, coast guard, and marines.

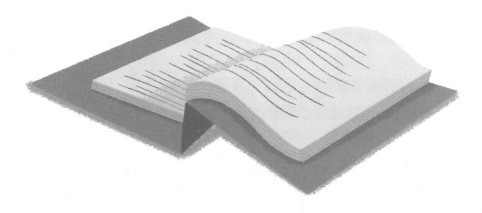

In Congress, Shirley worked to get more funding for day care programs for children of working parents. She wanted equal rights for women, better healthcare, and greater opportunities for poor and working families. In her very first speech in the House of Representatives on March 26, 1969, she spoke out against the Vietnam War and promised to vote against bills that gave more money to the war instead of helping the people of the United States.

It was because she fought for them that working people around the country supported Shirley in running for president. An African American woman had never sought the presidential nomination from either the Democratic or Republican party before. But that didn't bother Shirley.

On January 25, 1972, at the Concord Baptist Church in Brooklyn, New York, Shirley announced she was running for president of the United States.

Chapter 4
"Candidate of the People"

"I am not the candidate of black America, although I am black and proud," Shirley said when she announced she was running for president. "I am not the candidate of the women's movement of this country, although I am a woman, and I'm equally proud of that. . . . I am the candidate of the people of America."

From the beginning, Shirley's campaign was an uphill battle. She had a lot less money than the men she was running against. Many people treated her campaign like a joke.

Even though Shirley met with a lot of obstacles, she didn't give up. She didn't win enough votes in the Democratic primaries to be the party's nominee, but she became the very first African American woman to have her name entered as a nominee at the Democratic National Convention. The Democratic and Republican National Conventions are where each party decides on who their nominee for president shall be. The party also decides on a statement on what the president's goals will be should he or she be elected. This party statement is known as a **platform**.

George McGovern won the Democratic Party's nomination and lost the November election to President Richard Nixon, who was the Republican candidate.

Shirley believed that her campaign would make it possible for more women and more African Americans to run for president, and to be taken seriously. "The door is not open yet, but it is ajar," she said.

Chapter 5
Dare to Dream

After the election, Shirley got back to work in Congress. She continued to fight for the causes she believed in and to work with other representatives to pass laws.

Shirley served a total of fourteen years in Congress before she decided to retire in January 1983.

She left Congress, but Shirley didn't give up the fight. She taught politics at Mount Holyoke College in Massachusetts and cofounded a political group for black women. She also remained active in the Democratic Party and worked on other candidates' campaigns.

In 1993, President Bill Clinton asked Shirley to be the US ambassador to Jamaica, but by that time she was in poor health. She lived a quiet life in Florida until she passed away on January 1, 2005.

The world continues to be inspired by Shirley. In 2015, President Barack Obama awarded her with the Presidential Medal of Freedom after her death. And in 2020, she became the first woman to have a public statue dedicated to her in  Brooklyn. The forty-foot-tall structure combines a statue of Shirley with an image of the United States Capitol building. Seats around the statue will bear the names of women who have followed in her footsteps and been elected to the US Congress.

Shirley would be proud of those honors. She would be even more proud of the inspiration she became for women and men all over the world who dreamed of running for political office and thought perhaps they couldn't or shouldn't pursue their dream.

Shirley Chisholm had the courage to dream. She had the courage to stand up for change. Now that you've met her, don't you think you can do the same?

BUT WAIT . . .

THERE'S MORE!

Turn the page to learn about the three branches of the US federal government and how voting works!

41

The United States Government

One thing that makes the United States government special is that it is made up of three different branches. This is deliberate, so no one branch can make all the decisions. The founders of the United States wanted to make sure no group or single person in our government could become too powerful.

The three branches of government are the **executive branch** (the president, the vice president, and the cabinet), the **legislative branch** (the House of Representatives and the Senate), and the **judicial branch** (the Supreme Court).

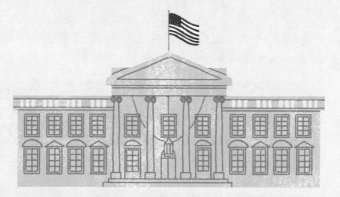

The Executive Branch

The leader of the executive branch is the president of the United States. All the other members of this branch of government report to the president. The president gets advice and help from the vice president and department heads (called **members of the cabinet**). Cabinet members give advice to the president on issues and help carry out decisions made by the government. The president is elected by United States citizens and carries out the laws of the land and leads the military. The vice president becomes president if the president can no longer do the job.

To ensure that the president does not have too much power or control, a person is limited to two four-year terms of being president of the United States.

The Legislative Branch

The legislative branch, called **Congress**, is made up of two parts: the House of Representatives and the Senate. Congress is in charge of making laws. The members of the House of Representatives and the Senate are voted into office by American citizens in each state.

The Judicial Branch

The judicial branch is in charge of defining or interpreting our laws, how the laws apply to situations in real life, and whether or not a law breaks any rules of the **Constitution**. The Constitution was written by the founders of the United States in 1787 and became the highest form of law in the country in 1788. The Constitution created our three branches of government and describes how each branch works.

The United States Supreme Court is part of the judicial branch. It is the highest court in the country. The Supreme Court is made up of nine judges (called **justices**) who are nominated by the president and confirmed by the members of the Senate. Once a person becomes a Supreme Court justice, that is their job for life unless the justice wishes to retire early. Why do they get their job for life? It's to make sure they are making decisions based on their conscience, not to get reelected.

The job of the courts is to interpret the laws of Congress. They do not *make* laws. Once the Supreme Court makes a decision in a case, the decision can be changed only by a later Supreme Court decision, or by changing—or **amending**—the Constitution.

Voting

Voting is an important process in our government. Voting allows you to exercise your rights as a citizen of the United States by choosing a representative or policy that best matches your views.

Voting by the Numbers in the United States

You must be eighteen years old or older to vote.

There are two main political parties in the United States. They are the Republican and Democratic Parties.

Presidential elections are held every four years.

Elections to the United States Senate are staggered and are held every two years. A senator's term of office is six years. The full United States House of Representatives elections are held every two years.

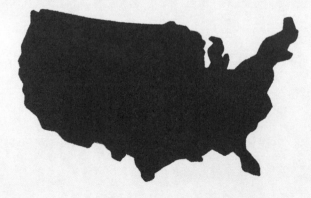

Now that you've met Shirley, what have you learned?

1. How often are presidential elections held?
a. every 6 years   b. every 2 years   c. every 4 years

2. How long is a senator's term of office?
a. two years   b. six years   c. for life

3. Who was the first African American woman elected to the US Congress?
a. Shirley Chisholm   b. Rosa Parks   c. Sojourner Truth

4. Why is voting important?
a. It's a way to exercise your rights.
b. You can make your voice heard.
c. It's an opportunity to choose representatives or policies that best match your views.
d. all of the above

5. Shirley Chisholm once said, "If they don't give you a seat at the table, bring a folding chair." What did she mean?
a. Find a way to be seen and heard even if people try to discourage you.
b. Bring your own chair everywhere so you will be comfortable.
c. Folding chairs are easy to carry.
d. Don't sit on the floor. Your clothes will get dirty.

6. Shirley's campaign slogan was "Unbought and Unbossed." What did that mean?
a. She didn't buy any new clothes for the campaign.
b. She let other people tell her what to do.
c. She hadn't taken money from big corporations, and no one could tell her what to do.
d. She liked bossing other people around.

7. Who did Shirley say she was the candidate for?
a. black Americans   b. women
c. the American people   d. young mothers

8. What was dedicated to Shirley Chisholm in 2020 to honor her memory?
a. a book   b. a statue
c. a song   d. a poem

Answers: 1.c 2.b 3.a 4.d 5.a 6.c 7.c 8.b